Original title:
Snooze in the Moonlight

Copyright © 2024 Creative Arts Management OÜ
All rights reserved.

Author: Julian Montgomery
ISBN HARDBACK: 978-9916-90-730-6
ISBN PAPERBACK: 978-9916-90-731-3

Tranquil Time Between Stars

In the stillness of the night,
Whispers of dreams take flight.
Silvery beams softly gleam,
Cradling a lonesome dream.

The cosmos hums a sweet tune,
Underneath the watchful moon.
Each twinkle a promise made,
In the vast, celestial shade.

Gentle breaths of stardust breeze,
Rustling softly through the trees.
Moments paused in starry glow,
Time flows quietly, soft and slow.

Lost in thoughts as shadows wane,
Carried on a cosmic plane.
In tranquil time, hearts align,
Between the stars, love will shine.

The Night's Embrace

Whispers of shadows softly creep,
Under the moon, the world is deep.
Stars like jewels in velvet sky,
In the darkness, hearts can fly.

Dreams entwined in a silken thread,
Where the weary lay their heads.
A gentle hush, a lullaby,
The night's embrace, a gentle sigh.

Gentle Tides of Rest

Waves that kiss the sandy shore,
Secrets whispered evermore.
Breezes dance with twilight's glow,
As the day begins to slow.

Stars emerge, a twinkling sea,
Cradling souls in harmony.
Like a dream, the night unfolds,
Gentle tides where love beholds.

Essence of the Silver Night

In the stillness, a breath of light,
The essence of the silver night.
Moonlit paths where shadows play,
Guide the lost along their way.

Fingers weave through starlit air,
Carving memories with gentle care.
Each heartbeat a soft refrain,
In the night, a sweet domain.

Enchanted by Starlight

Glistening pearls above the trees,
Magic wrapped in a gentle breeze.
Each star whispers tales of old,
Promises in silver cold.

Hearts awaken, spirits soar,
Enchanted by the night's allure.
Together we'll dance through the dark,
Guided by dreams, igniting a spark.

Mystic Slumbers

In twilight's embrace, dreams softly weave,
Whispers of magic, hearts gently believe.
Shadows dance lightly, in the night's glow,
Mystic slumbers beckon, where secrets flow.

Stars shimmer above, like gems in the dark,
Touching the silence, igniting a spark.
In the realm of the dreamers, we find our way,
Lost in the beauty of night's ballet.

The Dream Weaver's Kiss

A tapestry spun with threads of the night,
The dream weaver's kiss brings visions of light.
Floating on clouds, where wishes take flight,
Every heartbeat echoes, pure love's delight.

Glimmers of starlight twirl in the air,
A soft lullaby sings, free from all care.
Capturing moments, both tender and sweet,
In the embrace of dreams, our souls meet.

Radiant Nightfall

As shadows unfurl, the horizon gleams,
Draped in the colors of twilight's dreams.
A canvas of wonder, painted with grace,
Radiant nightfall grants a soft embrace.

The moon's gentle glow lights the silent sky,
Stars whisper secrets, let spirits fly.
In the hush of the evening, time stands still,
Under the night's watch, hearts softly thrill.

Driftwood Thoughts Under the Moon

On shores of reflection, where driftwood lies,
Thoughts float like whispers beneath midnight skies.
Carried by tides, memories collide,
Under the moon's glow, dreams come alive.

Waves murmur stories of love and of loss,
Each ripple a tale, each crest a cross.
Bathed in the silver, the world feels anew,
Driftwood thoughts linger, soft as the dew.

Moonlit Reverie

Beneath the silver glow, we stand slow,
Whispers of the night, a soft, sweet flow.
In the silence, secrets softly weave,
A tapestry of dreams we dare to believe.

The owls call a tune from branches high,
As stars blink down like a watchful eye.
Moonbeams dance on leaves, a gentle waltz,
In this stillness, we find our hearts' pulse.

Starlit Dreams Unfurled

In the expanse where wishes take flight,
We chase the shadows that linger in light.
A constellation born of whispered dreams,
Floating on air, like ephemeral streams.

Each twinkle a promise, each flicker a spark,
Guiding us gently through the deepening dark.
Hopes flare brightly in the cosmos above,
Kissing our fears with the warmth of love.

Tranquil Nocturne

A serenade sung in the hush of the night,
Soft melodies cradle us, holding us tight.
The breeze carries secrets from faraway lands,
As we listen to nature's soft, gentle bands.

Crickets provide a rhythmic embrace,
While moonlight bathes us in its silvery grace.
With each moment, the world fades away,
Leaving only peace until break of day.

The Calm Between Shadows

In the linger of dusk, where whispers unite,
Shadows stretch long, welcoming the night.
Between the light and the dark, we find joy,
In fleeting moments that time can't destroy.

The twilight holds secrets, both tender and wise,
As the horizon blushes, painting the skies.
Here in the calm, where our worries subside,
We breathe in the stillness, our hearts open wide.

Rest Beneath Celestial Light

Under the stars, we lie so still,
Dreams entwined with the moonlight's thrill.
Soft whispers of night, a gentle embrace,
In this tranquil haven, we find our place.

Stardust dances on the cool, calm air,
We float through the silence, without a care.
Silver beams weave through night's quilted frame,
In the celestial glow, we are but a flame.

Swaying with the Night Breeze

The trees sway slow, a soft lullaby,
Carried along by the night's gentle sigh.
Petals flutter down, kissed by the air,
Whispers of secrets, the moon's silver glare.

Crickets are singing beneath the vast sky,
Filling the stillness with voices that fly.
As shadows cascade upon silvery grass,
We dance in the twilight, let moments amass.

Midnight's Tender Caress

Midnight descends with a soft, sweet breath,
Cradling the world in its arms, like death.
Stars blink awake, their promise of light,
Guiding the lost through the heart of the night.

With every tick, the night softly hums,
Echoes of dreams and of distant drums.
Hearts beat in rhythm, a gentle refrain,
Lost in the moment, we rise to the pain.

Quietude in the Night's Archive

In the archives of night, silence prevails,
Where stories of shadows weave delicate tales.
Fragments of memories float through the air,
Whispers of hearts that once lived bare.

A canvas of stars spreads wide above,
Painting the dreams we dare to love.
In this quietude, we softly abide,
Finding our peace in the night's gentle tide.

Between the Night's Soft Veil

In quiet dreams the shadows play,
Stars whisper secrets, night holds sway.
A tranquil hush wraps around tight,
Embracing all within its light.

The moonlight dances on the ground,
Silent echoes, a soothing sound.
Lulled by the softest sighs of night,
We drift away till morning's light.

Shadows of Sweet Escape

Beneath the trees where whispers dwell,
A hidden path, a secret shell.
With every step, the world retreats,
In shadow's grasp, my heart still beats.

The fragrance of the wild blooms near,
In twilight's glow, there is no fear.
I chase the dusk, the fading sun,
As day surrenders, night's begun.

Celestial Cradle

Cradled softly in the stars,
Light drifts gently, near and far.
Time suspends, the cosmos sighs,
In this embrace, the spirit flies.

Galaxies hum their tender song,
In stardust dreams, we all belong.
Each heartbeat blends with cosmic grace,
In the cradle of this infinite space.

Echoes of the Moonbeam Whisper

Beneath the glow of silver light,
Whispers of dreams take graceful flight.
Every beam tells tales untold,
In the night's embrace, we watch unfold.

Softly dancing in the breeze,
Nature's muse brings hearts to ease.
The echo lingers, sweet and clear,
In moonbeam whispers, love draws near.

Lullabies Beneath Silver Skies

Softly hum the night so bright,
With twinkling stars that guide our flight.
In dreams we weave our hopes anew,
Where peace and love will carry you.

Close your eyes, let worries fade,
In twilight's grasp, no debts are made.
The moon's glow lights our gentle way,
As dreams unfold in soft ballet.

Dreaming on Celestial Clouds

High above in endless blue,
We drift upon the dreams we grew.
With cotton candy whispers light,
We'll float through soft and starry night.

Each thought a star, each wish a breeze,
Cradled gently among the trees.
In this realm where silence reigns,
Our hearts will dance without the chains.

Whispers of the Night's Embrace

Hush now, hear the soft night call,
A soothing balm to cradle all.
In shadows deep, let secrets spill,
As dreams collide with silent will.

Stars twinkle bright, their stories old,
In every shimmer, warmth unfolds.
Together in this hush we find,
The treasures hidden in the mind.

Slumber's Dance Under the Stars

Beneath the veil of cosmic glow,
We twirl in dreams that gently flow.
Each heartbeat syncs with moonlit streams,
In slumber's dance, we weave our dreams.

The nightingale sings a lullaby,
As silver wings in darkness fly.
With every breath, we drift away,
Embraced by night until the day.

Morning's Prelude to Night

The sun dips low in the sky,
As hues of orange begin to die.
Whispers of the day grow faint,
Painting shadows, soft and quaint.

Crickets sing their twilight song,
As nature hums where we belong.
The breeze breathes secrets in the air,
A gentle call to dreams laid bare.

The Silent Heartbeat of Night

In the hush, the stars ignite,
A tapestry of silent light.
Each twinkle tells a tale of old,
A promise wrapped in silver cold.

The moon hangs low, a watchful eye,
Guarding dreams that flutter by.
In the stillness, whispers creep,
As the world succumbs to sleep.

Moonshadow Murmurs

Beneath the glow of pale moonlight,
Figures dance in the soft twilight.
Shadows play in secret glee,
Holding stories yet to be.

The night air carries soft sighs,
Echoes from the starlit skies.
In their embrace, we find our way,
Through the night till break of day.

Canvas of Celestial Dreams

Stars are brushstrokes on the night,
Crafting visions, pure delight.
Each dream a color, bright and bold,
In the gallery of stories told.

The cosmos weaves its splendid art,
Igniting wonder in the heart.
On this canvas, we take flight,
Exploring realms beyond our sight.

Under the Gaze of a Sleeping Universe

In stillness wrapped, the cosmos sighs,
A velvet hush beneath the skies.
Infinite dreams in silence weave,
Under the gaze, night takes its leave.

Wonders linger in the night,
Stars adore the soft moonlight.
Galactic whispers softly play,
As the universe fades away.

Stars Humming Lullabies to the Dreamer.

In the cradle of the night,
Stars weave tales, a soft delight.
Each shimmer sings a tender tune,
Lulling dreams beneath the moon.

Gentle glow, a guiding light,
Caressing hearts through tranquil night.
Whispers float on midnight air,
As hope awakens everywhere.

Whispers of Slumbering Stars

Stars asleep, in dreams they hide,
Carrying secrets, vast and wide.
In the quiet, soft words flow,
From the skies, where wonders grow.

Echoes drift through endless space,
A cosmic song, a warm embrace.
In tender twilight's gentle veil,
Starlit wishes softly sail.

Dreams Under Silver Beams

Silver beams in a tranquil night,
Cradle dreams in soft moonlight.
Floating whispers grace the air,
As fantasies drift without a care.

Crimson skies turn to deep blue,
Nurturing thoughts that feel so true.
In each moment, softly gleam,
As the world wraps around a dream.

The Stillness Before Dawn

Silhouettes dance in the hush,
Whispers of night, soft and rushed.
Stars flicker like secrets untold,
Awaiting the sun's gentle hold.

Time stands still in this breath,
An echo of life, a pause before death.
The world cradles dreams in sweet care,
Suspended in twilight's gentle air.

In the Arms of a Dream

In shadows the dreamers reside,
With wishes and hopes, they confide.
Floating on clouds of soft light,
Lost in the magic of night.

They chase the dawn with eyes closed tight,
Embraced by the lull of starlit flight.
Every heartbeat a whisper of grace,
In the arms of dreams, we find our place.

Tidal Waves of Lullabies

Gentle tides of melody sway,
Carrying the worries away.
Each note, a breath, a soft embrace,
Cradled in the moon's calming space.

Waves of sound, a soothing balm,
A symphony crafted to calm.
In the ocean of night, we drift free,
To the rhythm of love's timeless decree.

Nightbound Fantasies

In the realm where shadows play,
Fantasies weave and sway.
Whispers of magic fill the air,
For those who dream, life is rare.

Moonlit pathways call our name,
Adventures await in twilight's frame.
With every heartbeat, worlds align,
In the nightbound tales, we shine.

The Gaze of a Dreamer

In the quiet morn, visions rise,
Whispers of hope dance in the skies.
Eyes closed tight, the heart takes flight,
A world of shadows and beams of light.

Clouds of wonder drift and sway,
Each moment a canvas, bright and gay.
Threads of fate weave tales anew,
In the mind's embrace, each dream rings true.

Stars may fade, but dreams still bloom,
Within the heart, dispelling gloom.
With every breath, the spirit soars,
The gaze of a dreamer, forever explores.

In the twilight's glow, visions unfold,
Stories untold in colors bold.
Chasing the whispers of the night,
The dreamer's path shines ever so bright.

Ethereal Nightscapes

Under a veil of velvet skies,
Where the moon in slumber lies.
The world ignites with whispers soft,
Echoes of dreams that lift and loft.

Silhouettes dance, shadows sway,
Painting the night in a mystic play.
Stars like jewels in the dark expanse,
Invite the heart to lose in their trance.

Gentle breezes sigh and coo,
Nature's lullaby, sweet and true.
In this realm of celestial grace,
The night reveals its hidden face.

Time drips slowly in this sphere,
Moments linger, crystal clear.
Ethereal nightscapes wrap us whole,
Embracing the depths of the wandering soul.

Veiled in Moonlight Dreams

In the hush of night where secrets dwell,
Moonlight blankets all, casting its spell.
Whispers of slumber beckon near,
Veiled dreams shimmer, tender and clear.

Each beam a story, old yet new,
Reflecting desires, hopes that grew.
In silver shadows, the heart takes wing,
To realms of wonder, where spirits sing.

Gentle tides of thought arise,
Carried softly through starlit skies.
Within this haze, we find our way,
Guided by dreams that gently sway.

Veiled in moonlight, spirits dance,
Lost in the magic of night's romance.
The world asleep, but dreams awake,
In the tranquil night, our souls partake.

Hibernation in Starshine

Wrapped in the warmth of cosmic light,
We drift through depths of the endless night.
Stars like lanterns flicker and glow,
In this hibernation, time moves slow.

Beneath the shroud of the quiet sky,
The heart finds solace, the spirit can fly.
Clouds gather softly, a cradle of peace,
In the embrace of dreams, all worries cease.

Here in the stillness, we pause and sigh,
Letting the weight of the world float by.
In starshine's glow, we find our rest,
Awake in a slumber, forever blessed.

As galaxies spin in a silent waltz,
We hold our breath, yet never falter.
In this hibernation, we renew, revive,
In the dance of the cosmos, we truly thrive.

Astrological Wanderlust

Under starlit skies I roam,
Celestial bodies call me home.
Each constellation tells a tale,
In cosmic whispers, dreams set sail.

With every step on ancient ground,
In silence, magic can be found.
The universe, a vast expanse,
Invites my heart to take a chance.

Through galaxies, my spirit flies,
Chasing wonders in the skies.
In the night, I find my way,
As stardust dances, I will stay.

Delicate Flickers of Midnight

In the quiet of the night,
Soft light dances, pure delight.
Whispers float on the cool air,
Each moment crafted with care.

Moonbeams stitch the darkened seams,
Weaving softly in our dreams.
Delicate flickers, shadows play,
In the stillness, hopes find way.

Night unfolds its velvet cloak,
While the heart begins to soak.
In twilight's arms, we find our peace,
As time surrenders, worries cease.

Glimmers of Tranquility

Upon the lake, the sun's soft hue,
Reflects in silence, pure and true.
With gentle waves, the world stands still,
Embracing calm, the heart can fill.

Nature's breath, a soothing balm,
In every rustle, there's a charm.
Birdsongs weave through leafy trees,
A melody carried by the breeze.

In tranquil moments, life reboots,
Fleeting thoughts like gentle roots.
As shadows stretch and day departs,
In glimmers, we mend our hearts.

Where Wishes Meet Slumber

In twilight's hush, the dreams arise,
Softly whispered, amidst the sighs.
Where wishes linger, softly land,
In the cradle of night's gentle hand.

Stars align with a hopeful glow,
Carrying secrets only we know.
Each desire takes its flight,
Guided by the lull of night.

As sleep embraces, hearts unwind,
In slumber's realm, new paths we find.
Where wishes meet in silent prayer,
We journey forth without a care.

Moonbeams Cradling the Dreamer's Heart

In the silver glow, dreams take flight,
Cradled softly, in the night.
Whispers linger, shadows play,
Moonbeams guide the lost astray.

Hope dances in the cool night air,
Tender moments, free from care.
Stars painted bright across the dome,
In this quiet, we find home.

Lulled by lullabies from afar,
Each heartbeat syncs with every star.
In moonlit silence, hearts ignite,
Embraced by magic, pure and bright.

Sleep now drapes its velvet shroud,
Awakening dreams, sweet and loud.
For in this stillness, we shall find,
The secrets of the heart entwined.

Nighttime Whispers and Gentle Sighs

Underneath a velvet sky,
Softly sing the night's sweet sigh.
Stars converse in twinkling glow,
Tales of old, we long to know.

Each whisper floats on twilight air,
Guiding souls without a care.
Secrets shared in hushed refrain,
Combine to form a wistful chain.

While shadows dance and flickers fade,
Moonlight weaves through every glade.
Hearts align in gentle rhythms,
In the stillness, pure decisions.

As we drift in this embrace,
Finding peace in every space.
Nighttime wraps us in its wings,
Comfort found in whispered things.

The Embrace of Nocturnal Wanderlust

The stars invite a journey bold,
Wanderlust in dreams unfold.
Each step through shadows, dark yet bright,
Guided by the silver light.

The moon, a beacon in the night,
Calls to hearts that seek the flight.
Gentle breezes kiss the trees,
Whispering through the mysteries.

Across the lands of midnight's grace,
We chase the dreams we dare to face.
In every breath, a promise made,
Through cosmic paths, our hope won't fade.

Nocturnal dances sway and twine,
In every heartbeat, love aligns.
For in each moment, wild and free,
We find the depths of who we'll be.

Resting Places in Cosmic Light

In the glow of distant stars,
We find our solace, near and far.
Resting in the cosmic tide,
Where dreams and reality coincide.

Comets blaze through velvet skies,
A temporary paradise.
Each resting place, a gentle pause,
Invites reflection, just because.

Galaxies swirl with stories told,
Each flicker, bright, a life of gold.
Within the vast, we feel the seams,
Stitched together by our dreams.

In cosmic light, we shed our fears,
Cradled softly, through the years.
In rest we find our strength anew,
In every shine, a path to view.

Dreams Drift Through Lunar Haze

In shadows soft, the dreams do sigh,
Whispers weave as stars float by.
Each thought a cloud, a gentle trace,
In the stillness, we find our space.

The moonlight spills on quiet nights,
Guiding souls with silver lights.
A dance of hopes in midnight's breath,
Where wishes bloom, and fears meet death.

A tender touch of silken glow,
Invites the heart to take it slow.
Lost in the magic, we softly roam,
Finding solace, we are at home.

With every pulse, the silence calls,
Through lunar haze, where starlight falls.
In every dream that drifts away,
We linger long, till break of day.

Nocturnal Serenade of Stars

A symphony of night unfolds,
In hues of deep and stories told.
Each star a note, a shimmering line,
In cosmic rhythm, they intertwine.

The hush of night, a velvet cloak,
Beneath its weight, the worlds awoke.
With every twinkle, whispers soar,
In twilight's embrace, we seek for more.

The air is thick with dreams unspun,
As shadows dance until the sun.
A serenade that beckons near,
A melody that only night can hear.

So close your eyes and breathe it in,
Let the lullaby sink in within.
For in this hour, magic is found,
In nocturnal songs, we're spellbound.

Rest Beneath the Moon's Gaze

The moon hangs low with watchful eyes,
Casting dreams across the skies.
In silver beams, our worries fade,
Beneath its glow, a peace is made.

Soft whispers curl like autumn leaves,
In quietude that softly breathes.
Here in the night, we find our rest,
In lunar light, we're truly blessed.

Each sigh a star that lights the dark,
As night unfolds its gentle arc.
Cocooned in calm, we drift away,
In the moon's gaze, we long to stay.

With every heartbeat, time slows down,
In this stillness, we wear no crown.
For in this moment, all is clear,
Resting beneath the moon's soft cheer.

Sleeping in the Light of Night

In twilight's arms, we softly fade,
Beneath the stars, our dreams are laid.
The night whispers secrets we can't see,
In slumber's hold, we wander free.

A blanket woven from shadowed skies,
Cocooned in peace, no goodbyes.
With every breath, the world slows down,
As night enfolds with velvet gown.

The moon casts shadows, gentle and light,
Guiding our way through the depths of night.
In dreams we soar, on starlit waves,
Transported far to celestial caves.

Hold tight to dreams as they drift and glide,
In the light of night, we safely bide.
Awake to find the dawn so bright,
But for now, we sleep in the light.

Lunar Lullabies

Whispers of the night light,
Crickets sing their sweet tune,
Silver beams dance gently,
Under the watchful moon.

Night wraps the world in peace,
Clouds drift with a soft sigh,
Stars twinkle like soft dreams,
As time quietly slips by.

In shadows, dreams are born,
Cool breezes softly sway,
The heart finds its solace,
As night steals breaths away.

Sleep comes on whispered wings,
Cocooned in quiet grace,
Embraced by the night sky,
In a soft, warm space.

Night's Gentle Embrace

The stars blink in delight,
Cradled in dark's embrace,
While the world whispers low,
In a calm, dreamy space.

Branches bow down gently,
To the lull of the breeze,
Nature hums a sweet tune,
Inviting soft reprieves.

Moonlight spills like silk threads,
On slumbering hills so deep,
Where shadows weave small tales,
And starry promises keep.

Rest now, weary traveler,
Let go of the long day,
In night's gentle cradle,
Allow your dreams to play.

Serenade of the Sleepy Sky

The evening sky unfolds,
In hues of deep indigo,
As lullabies take flight,
On wings of twilight glow.

Celestial notes will soar,
Each star a twinkling chord,
Singing sweetly to the night,
A melody adored.

Clouds drift like soft whispers,
Through this tranquil expanse,
Inviting all to close eyes,
And join in the night's dance.

So breathe in this calm night,
Let your mind gently roam,
Wrapped in the serenade,
Of the sky, your true home.

A Soft Glow of Rest

A gentle light appears,
In the dark's tender fold,
Promising peace and dreams,
In a hue soft and gold.

The night is a warm blanket,
Embracing every soul,
Inviting tired hearts,
To surrender and be whole.

Time slows its quickened pace,
Under the moon's soft gaze,
While shadows play and dance,
In a quiet, dreamy haze.

Rest now, dear wanderer,
In the night's tender hold,
Let your dreams roam free,
As the world turns to gold.

Tranquil Shadows in the Evening Glow

In the hush of twilight's grace,
Shadows stretch and softly trace,
Whispers dance on gentle breeze,
Nature hums its sweet reprise.

Stars emerge to light the sky,
As the day says its goodbye,
Crickets sing their evening tune,
Underneath the watchful moon.

Trees stand tall with arms out wide,
Embracing night as shadows glide,
In this peace, the heart can rest,
Finding solace in the best.

Here, where time begins to slow,
In the tranquil evening glow,
Life's worries fade, love takes flight,
In the stillness of the night.

Moonlit Reverie of Wandering Souls

Beneath the moon's soft silver glow,
Wandering souls begin to flow,
Hearts entwined in silent dreams,
Lost in thought, or so it seems.

Each shadow speaks a secret song,
Where the night whispers belong,
In the silence, voices rise,
Underneath the starlit skies.

Footsteps dance on paths unknown,
In the darkness, seeds are sown,
Hope and longing find their place,
In this moonlit, sacred space.

Veils of night wrap round the heart,
As the journey plays its part,
With every breath, the soul takes flight,
In the reverie of night.

Chasing Nightfall's Gentle Breath

As the sun dips low and fades,
Nightfall casts its velvet shades,
Whispers travel on the air,
Painting dreams that linger there.

Stars ignite like tiny sparks,
Guiding hearts in shadowed parks,
In the stillness, secrets weave,
In the night, we dare believe.

Chasing echoes of the day,
Letting burdens drift away,
Bated breath in twilight's trance,
In the moonlight, we will dance.

With each moment, time stands still,
In this quiet, endless thrill,
Chasing nightfall, soft and sweet,
Where the world feels most complete.

Silken Slumber in Twilight's Arms

Embers fade as day departs,
Silken slumber tugs at hearts,
In twilight's arms, we softly melt,
Wrapped in peace that gently felt.

Clouds drift lazy, painted gold,
Every story waiting told,
In the cozy blanket night,
Dreams take flight on whispered sight.

Time slows down, the world retreats,
Where the heart and stillness meets,
In the shadows, candles glow,
Illuminating love we know.

Cradled by the night so deep,
In its arms, we drift to sleep,
Silken whispers guide our way,
Till the dawn brings forth the day.

Beneath a Blanket of Celestial Dust

Stars whisper softly in the night,
While galaxies spin in silent flight.
A tapestry woven by cosmic hands,
Each twinkle a story from distant lands.

Moonlight bathes the world in silver hue,
Casting shadows where dreams come true.
Beneath the vast sky, hearts start to trust,
Finding solace in celestial dust.

Dreamers gather, their hopes intertwined,
As nebulas dance, their colors unconfined.
In this realm where the universe sings,
Peace and wonder, the joy that it brings.

In the stillness, the cosmos unfolds,
Mysteries hidden, yet waiting to be told.
Beneath a blanket of stars we drift,
In the night's embrace, we find our gift.

Ethereal Refuge in Night's Embrace

In the hush of the night, dreams take flight,
Wrapped in shadows, the world feels right.
The moon a guardian, soft and wise,
Watching over with silvered sighs.

Whispers of night breeze, gentle and sweet,
Guide the weary on soft, padded feet.
Stars like lanterns gleam overhead,
Leading all wanderers safely to bed.

In this refuge, where silence prevails,
Every heartache and worry gently exhales.
Wrapped in twilight's comforting glow,
We find our peace, as the night winds blow.

Ethereal moments in starlight unfold,
Stories unspoken, but timelessly told.
Nestled beneath the velvet sky,
In the night's embrace, we learn to fly.

Wandering through the Dreaming Stars

Eager hearts wander, drifting afar,
Guided by light from a single star.
Through nebulous paths, our spirits ascend,
As whispers of twilight in the cosmos blend.

Secrets await in the silence profound,
Each step a journey, no boundaries found.
Eclipsing fears beneath cosmic veils,
With every heartbeat, a dream unveils.

We leap, we twirl in the stellar dance,
Everything shimmering, lost in a trance.
Galaxies beckon, come join in the play,
Wandering through dreams, we drift and sway.

With starlit graces that light up the night,
Endless horizons filled with pure delight.
In the vastness of heaven, we dare to roam,
Finding our stars, we create our home.

Serene Moments in the Lunar Glow

Under the canopy of a midnight sky,
Luna's embrace, a soft lullaby.
Her glow paints the world in gentle beams,
Inviting hearts to bask in their dreams.

Whispers of night float through the air,
Every sigh holds a memory rare.
In her light, all shadows softly fade,
Revealing the beauty in dusk's parade.

Time stands still in this tranquil space,
Each moment cherished, a sweet embrace.
With every heartbeat, peace starts to flow,
In serene moments, as the moon's face glows.

Lost in reflections, the world drifts away,
Under the moonlight, we dance and sway.
In harmony bathed by this luminous show,
Finding our solace in the lunar glow.

The Sigh of Celestial Dreams

In the hush of twilight's grace,
Whispers of stars begin to trace.
Dreams take flight on silver beams,
Lost in the sigh of celestial dreams.

Gentle winds through branches sway,
Carrying thoughts of night's ballet.
Waves of peace in shadows gleam,
Held close within celestial dreams.

Starlight's Gentle Invitation

Above, the cosmos breathes divine,
Stars twinkle soft in a cosmic line.
Each flicker holds a story's span,
In starlight's gentle invitation.

Moonlight spills on slumbered ground,
A serene peace in silence found.
Gathered moments in night's embrace,
Allured by starlight's gentle grace.

Resting in the Night's Arms

Embraced by night with tender care,
Stars a blanket, dreams to share.
Resting low where shadows play,
In the night's arms, we drift away.

Softly hums the cool night breeze,
Whispers dance among the trees.
In this bliss, our spirits glow,
Resting in the night's warm flow.

Visualizing the Quiet Moon

A canvas painted deep in blue,
With silver edges, soft and true.
The quiet moon begins to rise,
Visualizing a world in sighs.

Below, the earth in silence lays,
Bathed in cool, serene moon's rays.
Dreams awaken in twilight's boon,
Gazing upon the quiet moon.

Lull of the Nightingale

In the hush of evening's grace,
A nightingale finds its place.
With melodies soft and light,
It whispers dreams into the night.

The moon drapes silver on the ground,
While symphonies in shadows found.
Songs of love and tranquil sighs,
In the stillness, hearts arise.

Stars twinkle like distant eyes,
As nightingale softly cries.
Each note a tender serenade,
In twilight's gentle masquerade.

With every pulse of night's embrace,
Fades the day without a trace.
Let the lull of nature reign,
In the night's sweet, soft refrain.

A Reverie in Silence

In the stillness, thoughts take flight,
Drifting softly, a feathered light.
Whispers linger in the air,
In reverie, I find the rare.

Time slips by, a gentle stream,
As I wander through a dream.
Moments stretch, then fade away,
In this quiet, I long to stay.

A world untouched by noise or rush,
Where silence echoes, hearts can hush.
In the calm, I breathe and grow,
Letting go of all I know.

In twilight's realm, my spirit soars,
Through open windows, timeless doors.
A reverie spun in sacred space,
Where silence finds its warm embrace.

Beneath the Ethereal Dome

Underneath the vast expanse,
Stars perform their ancient dance.
Galaxies twirl in cosmic light,
Painting dreams against the night.

A tapestry of twilight hues,
Wraps the earth in mystic views.
Gentle breezes carry song,
As the universe hums along.

With every heartbeat, whispers soar,
Secrets hidden, legends roar.
In this magic, hearts ignite,
Lost in wonder, pure delight.

Beneath this ethereal dome,
We find ourselves, we find our home.
In starlit paths, our spirits roam,
Together, here, we are not alone.

Stolen Moments Under the Stars

In twilight's glow, we find our place,
Stolen moments, a sweet embrace.
Underneath the twinkling sky,
Time stands still as we whisper why.

Our laughter dances on the breeze,
Carried far through ancient trees.
Every glance catches the light,
In the magic of this night.

Constellations tell our story,
As we bask in love's sweet glory.
In shadows deep, our wishes soar,
Stolen moments, who could ask for more?

Hand in hand, with stars above,
We weave our dreams, we find our love.
In the quiet, hearts aligned,
Stolen moments, forever entwined.

Stars Tucked Into Dreamscapes

Stars shimmer softly in the night,
Whispers of dreams take gentle flight.
Every twinkle hides a tale,
In cosmic realms where wishes sail.

Lunar glow paints shadows blue,
Guiding souls to what feels true.
Nestled in the velvet sky,
Hearts awaken, wandering high.

Restless thoughts drift far away,
In starlit paths where visions play.
A tapestry of hopes unspun,
Underneath the moon, we run.

With each dawn, the dreams may fade,
Yet in that dark, our hearts are swayed.
For every star that lights the night,
A piece of us takes flight, takes flight.

The Quietude of Night's Caress

In shadowed corners, silence gleams,
The world drifts softly into dreams.
Crickets sing their lullabies,
While stars unfold in endless skies.

Moonlit whispers brush the trees,
Carrying secrets on the breeze.
Time slows as the shadows sway,
In night's embrace, we find our way.

Glistening dew on blades of grass,
Moments linger, hours pass.
Each heartbeat syncs with nature's song,
In this quietude, we belong.

As night extends its tender reign,
We find solace in gentle pain.
For in the silence, truth we find,
A deeper peace, entwined, entwined.

Hush of the Evening Tide

The sun bows low, the day takes flight,
A symphony of colors ignites.
Waves whisper secrets to the shore,
As twilight calls, we long for more.

The horizon blushes, glowing gold,
Each ripple carries dreams untold.
In the hush, our thoughts align,
Nature's rhythm, pure and divine.

Stars awaken, one by one,
Dancing in the twilight run.
With every heartbeat, tide and land,
We feel the pull, we understand.

As night unfolds its calming shroud,
We lose our fears amidst the crowd.
For in the hush, we are alive,
Together, in this moment, we thrive.

Velvet Nightscapes of Slumber

Beneath the canopy of night,
Dreams weave pathways, pure delight.
In velvet folds, our worries hide,
As we surrender to the tide.

Pillow thoughts like clouds take flight,
Carried far by gentle night.
Stars are guides in realms we fly,
Unlocking worlds where spirits sigh.

Each heartbeat whispers, close your eyes,
Embrace the calm that gently lies.
In this space, our souls unite,
In velvet nightscapes, pure and light.

With dawn, the magic may recede,
Yet in the heart, the dreams still lead.
Though morning calls, we hold the key,
To endless nights of mystery.

Dreams of the Drowsy Sea

Waves whisper softly to the shore,
As the sun sinks low, inviting more.
Beneath the moon's gentle, silvery gleam,
The ocean cradles a tranquil dream.

Fishermen's boats sway in the breeze,
Their nets cast wide, aiming to please.
The tide rolls gently, a lullaby sweet,
In the embrace of a world discreet.

Stars twinkle above in a velvet sky,
Reflecting whispers of a bye-and-bye.
Each ripple holds secrets deep as night,
On this drowsy sea, everything feels right.

As I close my eyes, I drift away,
To a magical realm where dreams hold sway.
In the heart of the sea, I find my peace,
In the dreams of the drowsy, a sweet release.

The Serenity of Nightfall

The sun bows out with a golden flare,
Night blankets earth with tender care.
Whispers of dusk paint shadows long,
A soft embrace, a lullaby song.

Chirping crickets serenade the stars,
As the world fades under night's memoirs.
Moonlight dances on the silent lake,
In this calm hour, no hearts shall break.

Clouds drift lazily in twilight's hue,
Wrapping the world in a misty blue.
Dreams awaken as the shadows creep,
In the serenity, the tired sleep.

Magic unfurls in the still of night,
As the universe bathes in silver light.
In this peaceful hour, all is right,
Held in the arms of the gentle night.

Cradled in Starshine

In the quiet of night, stars gleam bright,
Whispers of cosmos fill hearts with light.
Each twinkle tells tales of ages past,
Lessons of love, in the universe cast.

Cradled by dreams, under heavenly glow,
Lost in the wonder, I silently flow.
Galaxies spiral in a dance so divine,
Guided by hopes, cradled in starshine.

The breeze carries secrets from afar,
Each breath of air, a wish on a star.
In this celestial tapestry's thread,
I find my solace, my fears shed.

Time stretches softly, a moment's embrace,
In the stillness, I've found my place.
With eyes closed tight, in dreams I align,
Forever cradled, lost in starshine.

Hush of the Twilight

Twilight descends like a whispered vow,
Nature holds its breath, in awe of the now.
Colors collide in a delicate blend,
As day meets night, a curve, a bend.

Crimson and purple, the sky softly weeps,
Gathering shadows in the land that sleeps.
Birds sing their last in melodious flight,
As the world surrenders to the hush of night.

Through rustling leaves, secrets are shared,
In the stillness, every heart is bared.
Moonlight, a painter, begins its soft stroke,
Wrapping each moment in silence bespoke.

The hush of the twilight whispers my name,
With each fleeting moment, things feel the same.
In the calm of the dusk, I find my way,
In the twilight's embrace, I long to stay.

Where the Cosmos Gently Naps

Where silence swells and whispers flow,
Stars twinkle softly, a heavenly glow.
Comets drift by on a gentle breeze,
The universe dreams beneath cosmic trees.

Planets spin slow in their tranquil dance,
Galaxies twirl, lost in a trance.
Time softly echoes in this serene sea,
Where the cosmos rests, wild and free.

Nebulas wrap in their colorful shrouds,
While moons watch o'er the sleeping crowds.
Dreams float on stardust, serene and bright,
In the hush of the cosmos, wrapped in night.

Here in the stillness of endless time,
Celestial beings hum rhythm and rhyme.
Where the cosmos napt, a peaceful embrace,
A moment forever in a timeless space.

Night's Heartbeat Under Starlit Firmament

Beneath the canvas of night's deep sigh,
Stars pulse in rhythm, like hearts close by.
The moon glimmers softly, a watchful gaze,
Guiding the dreams through the shadowy haze.

Crickets sing ballads in the cool night air,
Whispers of secrets, free from all care.
The world holds its breath in the tranquil dark,
Waiting for magic, a flickering spark.

Clouds drift slowly, a soft, gentle tide,
While night creatures wander, the wild as their guide.
The cosmos breathes deep as time gently flows,
In the heart of the night, where wonder bestows.

Wrapped in the stillness, the stars align,
With each quiet heartbeat, a grand design.
Under this firmament, we find our way,
In the quiet of night, our spirits shall play.

Resting on a Silvery Dusk

As day bows low, the sun bids goodnight,
A silvery dusk blankets the fading light.
Soft hues embrace the horizon's edge,
Whispers of twilight serenade the ledge.

A gentle breeze carries the scent of peace,
Where worries soften, and moments cease.
Golden rays mingle with shadows that play,
Resting on dusk as the night claims the day.

The stars awaken, one by one they shine,
Casting their glow in a heavenly line.
Dreams take flight on a lavender breeze,
In the hush of dusk, the soul finds its ease.

Each fleeting moment, like a cherished thought,
In the arms of twilight, all troubles forgot.
Resting with stars, under the velvet sky,
In the embrace of dusk, our spirits will fly.

Symphony of Sleep in Astral Dreams

In the quiet hours when the world fades away,
A symphony hums soft, leading hearts to sway.
We drift on melodies, woven with care,
In astral dreams, we forget all despair.

The night conducts with a luminous wand,
Creating a lullaby, gentle and fond.
Stars join in chorus, a celestial band,
As we sail through the cosmos, hand in hand.

Clouds become pillows where wishes take flight,
In whispers of starlight, we dance through the night.
With every heartbeat, the universe sings,
A lullaby woven with celestial strings.

Within this dreamscape, we find our release,
Wrapped in the rhythms of timeless peace.
In the orchestra of sleep, our souls entwine,
In symphony sweet, where the stars brightly shine.

Veil of Sleepy Nights

The stars emerge, a silent glow,
Soft whispers of the night winds flow.
Underneath the moon's embrace,
Dreams take flight in gentle space.

Shadows dance upon the ground,
In the silence, peace is found.
Curtains drawn, the world in hush,
Time slows down, in twilight's blush.

Clouds drift by, in pale array,
Night unfolds, and dreams convey.
Through the dark, the heart's delight,
Veiled in calm, the sleepy night.

In this realm, our senses fade,
Wrapped in warmth, our fears are laid.
Each breath soft, and deep, and free,
In the veil of night, we find the key.

Caressing Night's Whisper

Crickets sing a lullaby,
As silver beams adorn the sky.
In the stillness, shadows curl,
Tenderly, the night unfurls.

Stars like diamonds softly gleam,
Flowing gently in a dream.
Whispers float on midnight air,
Caressing thoughts beyond compare.

The world is wrapped in quiet peace,
All burdens cease, all troubles decrease.
Beneath the blanket of the dark,
Hope ignites a tiny spark.

Close your eyes; let worries part,
Feel the night embrace your heart.
In this moment, still and light,
Surrender to caressing night.

The Twilight Lull

When day gives way to night's embrace,
The twilight brings a gentle grace.
Colors blend in softest hues,
Painting skies with evening views.

The sun dips low, a golden ball,
While shadowed whispers softly call.
In this time, the world prepares,
For dreams to dance on evening airs.

The hush envelops, time stands still,
As stars awaken, hearts to fill.
A quiet peace descends like dew,
In twilight's lull, we breathe anew.

Crafting stories in the night,
Embracing all that feels just right.
A canvas wide, a heart that sings,
In twilight's glow, the magic brings.

Embracing Twilight Dreams

In the twilight's tender glow,
Dreams arise, like rivers flow.
Softly beckoning the night,
Embracing all with pure delight.

Stars awaken, one by one,
Guiding hearts till the night is done.
Gentle breezes start to sway,
As shadows dance and drift away.

Whispers linger, soft and light,
Holding secrets of the night.
In the twilight, hopes take flight,
A journey deep, beyond the sight.

Close your eyes and take the leap,
In this magic, safe and deep.
Twilight dreams await your call,
Embracing all, embracing all.

Shimmers of Rest

In twilight's embrace, we softly drift,
As whispers of dreams begin to lift.
Stars sprinkle the canvas, a gentle glow,
Here in the stillness, our worries slow.

The night's soothing breath brings peace anew,
Crickets hum softly, the world feels true.
Moonlight dances on leaves, silver threads,
We find our solace where silence spreads.

Gentle waves of slumber call our name,
In this calming realm, we lose our shame.
Time seems to pause, in this sacred space,
Wrapped in tranquility's warm embrace.

With hearts alight under the vast expanse,
We surrender to sleep, lost in a trance.
Dreams take flight on soft, feathered wings,
Hushed serenades of the night softly sing.

Echoes of a Serene Night

Beneath the canopy of endless stars,
Whispers ride the wind from afar.
Gentle rhythms of hearts in sync,
In the quiet night, we stop to think.

Each note of stillness, a tale untold,
As moonbeams glow with a hue of gold.
A symphony of silence, nature's art,
Echoes linger, melting the heart.

The cool breezes carry secrets deep,
Eager to share what they softly keep.
Night blooms open in splendid grace,
In every shadow, we find our place.

The universe listens, a watchful eye,
Holding our dreams as the hours fly.
In the serene night, love's whispers ignite,
Binding souls together, pure delight.

Beneath the Glare of Nebulas

Cosmic wonders spin in the blackened sea,
Painted in colors that set our spirits free.
Galaxies twirl, a dance of old,
Stories of time in the stardust told.

Beneath the glare, we ponder and gaze,
Caught in the magic of the nebula's haze.
Each twinkle a memory from ages past,
In this vast expanse, our questions cast.

Clusters of dreams shimmer overhead,
With hopes that linger, soft words unsaid.
Infinity stretches in every direction,
In cosmic silence, we find connection.

The universe hums softly, a lullaby,
Under its watch, we learn to fly.
With hearts wide open, we chase the light,
In the wonder of space, we feel so right.

Soft Shadows of Fading Light

As day gives way to gentle night,
Soft shadows gather, absorbing light.
Colors blend into a muted scene,
In the twilight glow, the world feels keen.

The horizon melts in hues of blue,
Embracing the darkness, a calming view.
Each breath we take, a whispered sigh,
As stars reveal themselves in the sky.

Figures emerge in silhouette form,
Dancing in rhythm, the night feels warm.
A tapestry woven with threads of peace,
In the embrace of dusk, our worries cease.

The world slows down, as shadows play,
In this gentle twilight, we wish to stay.
Cradled in stillness, we close our eyes,
Savoring moments as the daylight dies.

Occasions of Mellow Dreams

In the hush of night skies, soft whispers play,
Where shadows dance gently, and worries decay.
Stars blink like secrets, told in soft sighs,
Mellow dreams beckon, where tranquility lies.

Moments of peace wrapped in silken embrace,
Drifting on starlight, finding our place.
Time slows its ticking, gently we float,
In the ocean of slumber, our hearts take a note.

Colors of twilight paint the dreams we weave,
Enchanted by musings, we quietly believe.
With each soft breath, we journey afar,
Through occasions of dreams, like light from a star.

Awake in the dawn, with our hearts still aglow,
From mellowed adventures in night's gentle flow.
These whispers of dreams linger, tender and sweet,
In the echoes of night, where our souls softly meet.

A Sleepy Serenade

Softly the moon hums a lullaby tune,
Cradling the world beneath silvered swoon.
Waves of serenity ripple through the night,
As dreams take their flight, on the wings of delight.

With each gentle sigh, the stars start to gleam,
Wrapped in the fabric of a delicate dream.
Whispers of nightfall, so cozy and warm,
We drift on a current, a calming, sweet charm.

Dancing shadows linger, cast by the light,
Embracing the hush of this tranquil night.
In the arms of stillness, we find our refrain,
A sleepy serenade, where peace will remain.

So let the world fade as our eyelids grow heavy,
Nestled in slumber, hearts steady and ready.
Together we wander, through dreams we create,
In the symphony of night, we're destined to wait.

Twilight's Tender Soliloquy

In twilight's soft glow, where day meets the night,
   Whispers of colors blend warmly in flight.
   A soliloquy spoken in hues of bright gold,
     Bringing forth stories that softly unfold.

The breeze carries secrets from realms long unseen,
As shadows stretch longer, embracing the sheen.
Each moment a treasure, in silence we share,
   Awash in the magic of twilight's sweet air.

Hues shift and shimmer, as daylight takes rest,
A canvas of softness, nature's own quest.
In the heart of this hour, we find solace rare,
Twilight's gentle whispers cradle us with care.

And so we shall linger, wrapped in this charm,
Entwined in the echoes, forever disarm.
With twilight's embrace, we bid day adieu,
In this tender soliloquy, our hearts feel anew.

Between Dusk and Midnight

Between dusk and midnight, the world breathes a sigh,
Painted in shadows, where dreams softly lie.
The stars wink above, as the moon takes its throne,
Whispers of nightfall, feeling so much like home.

A canvas of silence, where thoughts drift like clouds,
Wrapped in the velvet of night's cozy shrouds.
Time dances softly, with moments so fleet,
Between dusk and midnight, our hearts find their beat.

Echoes of laughter in the cool evening air,
Carried by whispers, a sweet kind of prayer.
Together we wander, through this shimmering bliss,
In the magic of hours that we don't want to miss.

Crickets weave lullabies, as breezes collide,
Between dusk and midnight, we journey inside.
With hopes in our hearts and dreams in our eyes,
We linger in twilight where the soul truly flies.

Remnants of Daylight's Embrace

Golden hues fade from the sky,
Whispers of twilight gently sigh.
Shadows blend with fading light,
Anchoring dreams in the night.

Stars twinkle in soft delight,
Embers of day taking flight.
Memories woven, colors blend,
In the stillness, time can mend.

A world painted in twilight's charm,
Nature's pulse, a soothing balm.
In the grip of evening's spell,
Silent secrets begin to swell.

Holding on to what remains,
Fleeting joy and tender pains.
In daylight's dusk, we find our way,
Awakening dreams with the end of day.

The Art of Dreaming

In the silence of still night,
Minds take flight, reaching new heights.
Colors swirl in visions bright,
Crafting stories that feel so right.

Whispered thoughts in shadows dance,
Each moment a fleeting chance.
Words unspoken become the art,
Painting feelings from the heart.

With every breath, the soul takes wing,
In realms where hopes and visions sing.
Dreams entwined with starlit glow,
Guiding us where only we know.

Awake, we chase beyond the seams,
Holding tight to woven dreams.
For in the fabric of the night,
Lies the spark that brings forth light.

Floating on Moonlit Waves

Glistening waters under the moon,
Soft whispers of the ocean's tune.
Drifting gently, hearts so free,
Embraced by waves, just you and me.

Stars twinkle above, a guiding light,
Dreams unfurling in the night.
Each crest carries laughter's sound,
In this bliss, true love is found.

Moonlit paths where shadows play,
Cradled softly, the world slips away.
In the ebb and flow, we find our grace,
Time stands still in this sacred space.

Riding waves of silver light,
Together, we drift into the night.
Floating on the dreams we weave,
In this moment, we truly believe.

The Calm After Dusk

When the sun bows low, the calm arrives,
In the hush of night, tranquility thrives.
Gentle sighs of the weary world,
As darkness wraps its arms, unfurled.

Crickets sing their midnight song,
Nature's melody, soothing and strong.
In quiet corners, shadows nest,
A peaceful heart finds its rest.

The stars are scattered, diamonds so bright,
Guiding lost souls in the night.
With every breath, the calm restores,
Lifting spirits like ocean shores.

Time slows down in twilight's embrace,
Filling the void, a gentle grace.
Embracing stillness, surrendering fast,
In the calm, we find our past.